Deep Sea Creatures

KIDS EXPLORE!

Introduction

The earth is filled with oceans. And deep down below the surface of these bodies of water, lurk some really special creatures. Some of these are quite ugly and others can even be gruesome. However, the one thing they all have in common is they like the deep dark parts of their murky worlds. Let's dive into the deepest parts of the ocean to discover some of these amazing beasts. But beware... these creatures are really quite icky.

Viperfish

Did you know this fish is one of the oceans most ferocious predators? The Viperfish has long sharp teeth. In fact, its fangs are so big they can't fit inside its mouth. On the back of this deep sea creature is a long spine. On this spine's tip is a bioluminescent light. The Viperfish blinks this light on and off to lure its prey.

Giant Squid

Did you know this creature can be found a far as 3,280 feet (1,000 meters) below the surface of the ocean? The Giant Squid can reach 43 feet long (13 meters). Its body alone can measure around 6.6 feet (2 meters). This beast has 8 arms, 2 tentacles and a parrot-like beak it uses to catch and eat its prey.

Coffinfish

Did you know this fish can be found deep in the ocean off the East coast of Australia? The Coffinfish lives about 984.3 feet (300 meters) below the surface of the ocean. This odd fish only grows to be about 8.6 inches long (22 centimeters). It also has a flabby body with spines on it.

Fangtooth

Did you know this fish has the biggest teeth (in relation to its size) of all the ocean's fish? The Fangtooth fish is very gruesome indeed. But don't worry, it only grows to be about 6 inches long (16 centimeters). Along with its impressive set of chompers, it also has prickly scales covering its body.

Vampire Squid

Did you know this squid can be jet-black to a pale reddish color? The Vampire Squid lives about 3,500 feet (1,066 meters) below the surface of the ocean. This squid only grows to be about 6 inches in length (16 centimeters). Unlike other squids, the vampire squid has two fins on the top of it body. This helps it to move through the water.

Goblin Shark

Did you know out of all the sharks, this one may be the creepiest? The Goblin shark has a flabby body. It also has a trowel-like nose that sticks out quite far. The shark uses this to dig into the ocean floor. It has long needle-like teeth that it uses to crush its food of crabs, fish and shrimp.

Kelp

Did you know even plants grow deep in the ocean? This type of algae grows in what is known as 'kelp forests.' This type of plant can grow quite quickly. In fact, kelp can grow 1.6 feet (0.5 meters) each day! Full grown kelp can reach up to 260 feet tall (80 meters). Some sea creature will eat kelp and others hide among its flowing leaves.

Darth Vader Jellyfish

Did you know this jellyfish thrives in the cold arctic waters? The Darth Vader jellyfish was so named, because it looks like the evil Darth Vaders helmet from Star Wars. Not much is known about this jellyfish, but it does have 4 main tentacles and 4 smaller ones.

Dragonfish

Did you know this fish can make its own like? This is called, bioluminescence. The Dragonfish "lights up" around its mouth and on the end of its barbel. The female dragonfish can grow up to 15 inches long (40 centimeters) while the male only gets to be around 1.9 inches long (5 centimeters).

Attola Jellyfish

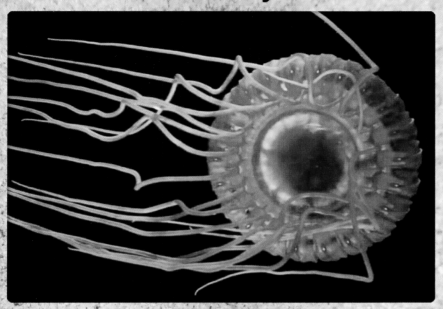

Did you know this jellyfish is deep red in color? The attola jellyfish has 22 tentacles and one really long tentacle. It is thought that the long tentacle helps this jellyfish hunt for food. This deep sea creature also has its own alarm system. When it is attacked, it launches a series of flashes. This attracts bigger predators that may just eat the attola's predator.

Posidonia oceanica

Did you know this is a sea grass found in the Mediterranean ocean? This plant forms large underwater meadows. It even has flowers and a fruit. These are free-floating and in Italy are called, "olives of the sea." When this sea grass washes up on shore it can form huge balls of dried debris on the beaches.

Long-nosed Chimaera

Did you know this creature has a long paddle-like nose? The Long-nosed Chimaera nose has tons of sensory nerve endings in it. This helps it find food. Its top fin is like a spine and is slightly venomous. It lives about 6,560 feet (,000 meters) under the water.

Gulper Eel

Did you know this bizarre creature has a huge mouth? The jaws of the Gulper Eel are hinged, so it can swallow fish and prey that is much larger than itself. This eel also has a pouch, like a pelican, where the food will sit before it is swallowed. The tip of the gulper's tail also has a pink light on it that can also glow red.

Deep Sea Angler

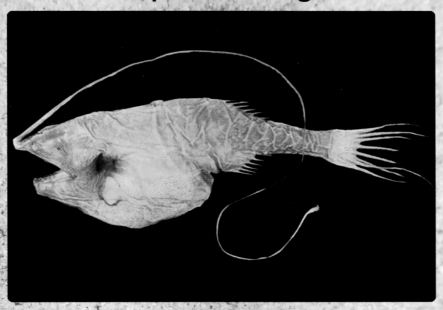

Did you know this fish has a long dorsal spine with a light on it? This is called, a photophore. The Deep Sea Angler is very round (something like a basketball) and has sharp, fang-like teeth. But don't worry, this fella only gets to be about 5 inches long (12 centimeters).

Giant Isopod

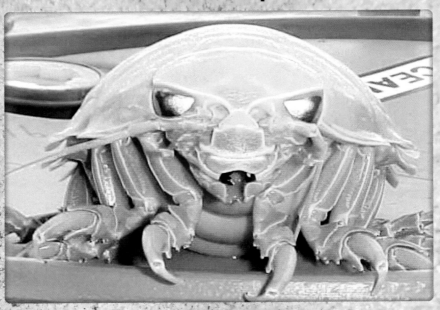

Did you know this deep sea critter looks like a giant bug? The Giant Isopod is actually related to shrimps and crabs. It can grow to be 16 inches long (40 centimeters). When this creature feels threatened it will roll itself into a tight ball. The eyes on this isopod also have over 4,000 facets!

Quiz

Question 1: Which deep sea creature can be found about 3,280 feet (1,000 meters) below the surface of the ocean?

Answer 1: The Giant Squid

Question 2: Which creature has a flabby body with spines on it?

Answer 2: The Coffinfish

Question 3: Which shark could possibly be the ugliest in the ocean?

Answer 3: The Goblin Shark

Question 4: Which sea plant grows flowers and a fruit?

Answer 4: Posidonia oceanica

Question 5: What is it called when a deep sea creature can make its own light?

Answer 5: Bioluminescence

Thank you for checking out another title from Kids Explore! Make sure to check out Amazon.com for many other great books.